Acceptance and Meaning in Grief

Wasyl Nimenko

Goalpath Books

Acceptance and Meaning in Grief

ISBN 978-1-908142-65-8

Published in Great Britain 2023

Copyright © Wasyl Nimenko 2023

Goalpath Books

Wasyl Nimenko was born in Ipswich and studied medicine in London, then psychotherapy.

Also by Wasyl Nimenko

Fiction   The Silent Guru and The Cave
Invisible Bullets

Non-Fiction   Carl Jung and Ramana Maharshi
Searching in Secret Ukraine
Notes from the Inside
The Spiritual Nature of Addictions

Travel   Searching in Secret Orkney
Searching in Secret India
Searching in Secret New Zealand and
Australia

Poems   The Fools Poems Part 1
The Fools Poems Part 11

The loss of someone you love

Can be like finding yourself in a powerful river

Where you have no control and no words

All you can do is keep afloat so you can breathe

Until the river becomes one with the sea

Goalpath Books

Acceptance and Meaning in Grief

GOALPATH BOOKS

1.

Acceptance and Meaning in Grief

CONTENTS

Normal Reactions to Abnormal Circumstances

Grief is one of the most powerful and difficult experiences of our life. There is no right or wrong reaction to loss because our grief is unique to us and we find our own individual way through it, with the help of others.

No one is an authority on grief. There are no words for grief and like the love that produces it; grief changes us and does not have an end.

There are a range of things we might experience which may not seem normal to us because they seem so foreign and strange to us, but they are normal reactions to abnormal circumstances. We all need help to get through our grief and sometimes we need help to know we are normal, are not going crazy or doing anything wrong. Grief can overwhelm us so that we get stuck and put our life on hold but it is only occasionally some of us need some extra help.

At first almost all of us are in shock. This varies from person to person and can last days, weeks, months or even years. We can feel numb and as if we are living in a different unreal world. We might see the person or hear them and speak to them which are all normal. This happens because we can forget they are dead, in-between trying to process that they have gone.

It is also normal to go over and over what happened to the person. We might feel anger or guilt over what we or others did or didn't do. It is normal to think what we or others could have, would have or should have done. We do not forget what happened but we can see it differently, especially if we talk about it. Some of us find it easy to cry and some of us don't. This is all normal adjusting.

We might think we can outrun grief by keeping busy doing things, such as keeping busy with work, shopping or housework. So, we keep running on adrenaline, thinking 'it won't catch me.' We might drink lots of tea or coffee, and then need alcohol to sedate us at night so that we can sleep. We can numb ourselves with lots of different things including alcohol, to fill the hole in our soul, to avoid being caught by grief.

Some of us can lose our appetite or find sleeping difficult. But the reverse can happen and we can overeat or sleep much more. We can feel low in our mood or very anxious and be more panicky. Our body can ache in pain. These are all normal in trying to adjust to what has happened to us and is happening to us.

∞

Unusually Difficult Grief

We may have no time to say goodbye and can be left feeling we have unfinished things to say to the person. This can happen if they died suddenly with no warning in an accident or by suicide or they had a very short illness like Covid.

At worst, our emotions can be fatal as in the occasional cases of severe grief which can cause 'Broken Heart Syndrome.' This has only recently become medically well recognised as 'Takotsubo Cardiomyopathy,' [1]

This problem is older than doctors realised. The impression that grief can damage the physical heart was first described in biblical times in the 8th century BC when Isiah said, 'He has sent me to bind up the broken hearted.' [2}

Some of us do not have opportunities to grieve with others at all because they may not understand our relationship with the person who has died. For example the death of an adopted person's birth parent they never met or the death of a 'non-blood' related person, or even a lover unknown to others. This may also be the case with a miscarriage or a stillborn child. This has come to be known as 'disenfranchised' grief. This also includes the death of pets. Losing someone can seem like an impossible thing to get through and so we need help and support from friends and family and everyone around us.

We also need a lot of listening to and understanding of ourselves by us and others over a long period of time. There may be practical things we can actually do to help us get through a particularly difficult loss.

Acceptance that we have lost someone can be the longest and most difficult part of grieving. At some moment we find and experience acceptance and see that we can carry on. However, sometimes we cannot find acceptance and grief can overwhelm us so that we get stuck and put our life on hold. Some of us may appear to grieve too much and this can be because the death and loss is unusually severe.

∞

Finding Acceptance With the Help of Others

A mother went to see a priest several months after her son committed suicide by jumping off a high building. She said that she was Catholic and believed her son had gone to Hell because he had committed a mortal sin by his suicide.

The priest said that maybe her son changed his mind whilst he was falling, in the last seconds of his life and had not wanted to die. Seeing this possibility, the mother was able to believe her son had changed his mind about killing himself and although he could not stop it, because he didn't want to die, he had not automatically gone to hell but was in heaven. Believing her son was not suffering she was able to accept his death.

Sharing what we believe and what are our deepest feelings can let others help us with their experience of death and loss in ways we might not have thought of.

∞

A young man was having more frequent moments of feeling sad about things. He couldn't put his finger on anything in particular or why he looked sad. He spoke with a therapist who asked about his parents who had divorced when he was a baby. His mother had died when he was eleven years old, but he only found out about his mother's death at the end of the week when it was announced in church. He was not allowed to go to the funeral and didn't know where his mother's grave was.

With encouragement from the therapist he found his mother's grave and held his own private ceremony there with flowers, fireworks, food and drink to celebrate his mother's life. He buried a long letter there to his mother, telling her about his life and saying goodbye. When he returned to see the therapist, he looked transformed with a beautiful smile and sounded like a different person.

Even when we have no way of going back in time and compensating for lost opportunities to grieve, this young man's story shows that we can create our own personal way of going through our grief.

∞

During Buddha's time, there lived a woman named Kisa Gotami. She married young and gave birth to a son. One day, the baby fell sick and died soon after. Kisa Gotami loved her son greatly and refused to believe that her son was dead. She carried the body of her son around her village, asking if there was anyone who can bring her son back to life.

The villagers all saw that the son was already dead and there was nothing that could be done. They advised her to accept his death and make arrangements for the funeral. In great grief, she fell upon her knees and clutched her son's body close to her body. She kept uttering for her son to wake up. A village elder took pity on her and suggested to her to consult the Buddha.

"Kisa Gotami. We cannot help you. But you should go to the Buddha. Maybe he can bring your son back to life!"

Kisa Gotami was extremely excited upon hearing the elder's words. She immediately went to the Buddha's residence and pleaded for him to bring her son back to life.

"Kisa Gotami, I have a way to bring your son back to life."

"My Lord, I will do anything to bring my son back"

"If that is the case, then I need you to find me something. Bring me a mustard seed but it must be taken from a house where no one residing in the house has ever lost a family member. Bring this seed back to me and your son will come back to life."

Having great faith in the Buddha's promise, Kisa Gotami went from house to house, trying to find the mustard seed. At the first house, a young woman offered to give her some mustard seeds. But when Kisa Gotami asked if she had ever lost a family member to death, the young women said her grandmother died a few months ago.

Kisa Gotami thanked the young woman and explained why the mustard seeds did not fulfil the Buddha's requirements.

She moved on to the second house. A husband died a few years. The 3rd house lost an uncle and the 4th house lost an aunt. She kept moving from house to house but the answer was all the same – every house had lost a family member to death. Kisa Gotami finally came to realise that there is no one in the world who had never lost a family member to death.

She now understood that death is inevitable and a natural part of life. Putting aside her grief, she buried her son in the forest. She then returned to the Buddha and became his follower. [3]

Perhaps listening to people from many households about death and loss let her see that although we experience loss uniquely, we are the same, as our loss is similar to everyone else's loss.

∞

A woman from the north of India had been swimming with her husband in the sea in Madras when in front of her eyes he was taken by a shark. She couldn't cope with it. She went everywhere seeing wise men and holy men to ask, 'What did we do wrong? Who did we harm? We married each other. We behaved correctly. Why?'

She had found that many people had talked to her, but when she went out, she couldn't remember what they had said. They had used long phrases about the soul and spirituality. She wanted an answer.

She visited the Osborne family in the southern town of Tiruvannamalai, whilst going to see the Indian sage Ramana Maharshi.

Katya Osborne, who was a young girl at that time recalls her experience and says that she couldn't bear sitting with the woman because she was tense and wound up. Katya was asked to take the woman to see Ramana Maharshi and she showed the woman into the Hall where Ramana Maharshi sat.

At the sound of the lunch time bell, Katya went to get her to take her back home. When she got back to the hall Katya saw the woman and still says. 'She was at peace and I couldn't belief it. I couldn't believe that this was the same women that I couldn't bear to be with a couple of hours ago. So I wanted to ask her what he had said because I thought to myself, whatever he had said to her

. . . those words must be the most important words in the World, they changed this woman completely, what are they, what did he say? I thought my mother will ask her, then I will find out. So we came home and my mother did ask her what she said and the woman answered.

'Nothing.' She had her list of questions which she took out. When he looked at her he looked so compassionate, she suddenly thought, 'It doesn't matter.' She left the list of questions and came out of the hall.

The silent look of compassion this woman received had such a profound effect on her that its impact was not only seen and felt by Katya when she collected her, but still is today when she tells her story to share with others on You Tube. [4]

Even in the presence of a person with a long list of questions, Ramana Maharshi chose to communicate as usual through silence. His silence needs some explanation because although it seems unusual, silence is well recognised as sometimes being one of the most important means of communication. Ramana Maharshi taught almost exclusively in silence. In the daily recorded dialogues over 4 years and 3 months, it can be seen that he only spoke on about 40% of the days and only spoke on average 165 words a day which by any standard is virtual silence. [5] In 1935 Ramana Maharshi outlined the origin of the use of silence:-

M.: . . . By silence, eloquence is meant. Oral lectures are not

12

so eloquent as silence. Silence is unceasing eloquence. The Primal Master, Dakshinamurthy, is the ideal. He taught his rishi disciples by silence. [6]

The English psychiatrist Anthony Storr [7] encouraged this type of communication in his last book 'Feet of Clay.' . . . if someone must seek a guru it is best to choose one who does not speak.

In chapter 56 of the Tao Te Ching, silence is regarded as a mark of primal union, the highest state of man.

Chapter 56

Those who know do not talk.
Those who talk do not know.

Keep your mouth closed.
Guard your senses.
Temper your sharpness.
Simplify your problems.
Mask your brightness.
Be at one with the dust of the earth.
This is primal union.

He who has achieved this state
Is unconcerned with friends and enemies,
With good and harm, with honour and disgrace.
This therefore is the highest state of man. [8]

∞

When Albert Einstein and Ramana Maharshi helped people in grief, what they said in their own way communicated the same error we have about being separate individuals.

Ramana Maharshi on another occasion speaks of grief.

M.: The birth of the 'I-thought' is one's own birth, its death is the person's death. After the 'I-thought' has arisen the wrong identity with the body arises. Thinking yourself the body, you give false values to others and identify them with bodies. Just as your body has been born, grows and will perish, so also you think the other was born, grew up and died. Did you think of your son before his birth? The thought came after his birth and persists even after his death. Inasmuch as you are thinking of him he is your son. Where has he gone? He has gone to the source from which he sprang. He is one with you. So long as you are, he is there too. If you cease to identify yourself with the body, but see the real Self, this confusion will vanish. You are eternal. The others also will similarly be found to be eternal. Until this truth is realised there will always be this grief due to false values arising from wrong knowledge and wrong identity. [9]

∞

Albert Einstein echoed this in replying to a letter in February 1950 from a rabbi who wrote to him for help as he was distraught at the death of his 11-year-old son from Polio.

Dear Dr. Einstein,

Last summer my eleven-year-old son died of Polio. He was an unusual child, a lad of great promise who verily thirsted after knowledge so that he could prepare himself for a useful life in the community. His death has shattered the very structure of my existence, my very life has become an almost meaningless void — for all my dreams and aspirations were somehow associated with his future and his strivings. I have tried during the past months to find comfort for my anguished spirit, a measure of solace to help me bear the agony of losing one dearer than life itself — an innocent, dutiful, and gifted child who was the victim of such a cruel fate. I have sought comfort in the belief that man has a spirit which attains immortality — that somehow, somewhere my son lives on in a higher world…

What would be the purpose of the spirit if with the body it should perish… I have said to myself: "It is a law of science that matter can never be destroyed; things are changed but the essence does not cease to be… Shall we say that matter lives and the spirit perishes; shall the lower outlast the higher?

I have said to myself: "Shall we believe that they have gone out of life in childhood before the natural measure of their days was full have been forever hurled into the darkness of oblivion? Shall we believe that the millions who have died the death of martyrs for truth, enduring the pangs of persecution have utterly perished? Without immortality the world is a moral chaos...

I write you all this because I have just read your volume The World as I See It. On page 5 of that book you stated: "Any individual who should survive his physical death is beyond my comprehension... such notions are for the fears or absurd egoism of feeble souls." And I inquire in a spirit of desperation, is there in your view no comfort, no consolation for what has happened? Am I to believe that my beautiful darling child... has been forever wedded into dust, that there was nothing within him which has defied the grave and transcended the power of death? Is there nothing to assuage the pain of an unquenchable longing, an intense craving, an unceasing love for my darling son?

May I have a word from you? I need help badly.

Sincerely yours,

Robert S. Marcus

A few days later Einstein sent a reply to the man who was a complete stranger.

February 12 1950

Dear Dr. Marcus:

A human being is part of the whole, called by us "Universe," a part limited in time and space. He experiences himself, his thoughts and feelings as something separated from the rest — a kind of optical delusion of his consciousness. The striving to free oneself from this delusion is the one issue of true religion. Not to nourish the delusion but to try to overcome it is the way to reach the attainable measure of peace of mind.

With my best wishes, sincerely yours,

Albert Einstein [10]

∞

Rumi the Sufi mystic expresses this unity in a poem . . .

Look at Love

look at love
how it tangles
with the one fallen in love

look at spirit
how it fuses with earth
giving it new life

why are you so busy
with this or that or good or bad
pay attention to how things blend

why talk about all
the known and the unknown
see how the unknown merges into the known

why think separately
of this life and the next
when one is born from the last

look at your heart and tongue
one feels but deaf and dumb
the other speaks in words and signs

look at water and fire
earth and wind
enemies and friends all at once

the wolf and the lamb
the lion and the deer
far away yet together

look at the unity of this
spring and winter
manifested in the equinox

you too must mingle my friends
since the earth and the sky
are mingled just for you and me

be like sugarcane
sweet yet silent
don't get mixed up with bitter words

my beloved grows right out of my own heart
how much more union can there be [11]

∞

Finding Meaning in Grief

Grief not only puts our loss and our own life in perspective but it also offers the opportunity to re-visit and review the meaning of our life. Our world may seem as if it is over and we might find it difficult to find a reason to carry on living. If we can find meaning in our grief, it protects us and our health both physically and mentally. Victor Frankl observed many times that the ones who survived the Holocaust of the German concentration camps were the ones who could find meaning. He supports Nietzsche's words, 'He who has a why to live can bear with almost any how.' [12]

Deciding if someone is likely to commit suicide is deemed much more unlikely if they have 'protective' factors in their life, such as close family or a project they need to finish That is they have meaning in their life. The principle of having enough meaning in their life to consider it worthwhile continuing living is used by all those assessing someone for suicidal risk.

It is not difficult to find 'meaning' in our own life, to have something or someone to live for. But trying to understand 'the meaning of life' is a different thing altogether. Perhaps this is best explained simply by the most highly regarded scientist and the most highly regarded sage of the last century.

Einstein says the aim is to stop seeing our self as being separated from the part of the whole, the "Universe." He calls it a kind of optical delusion of consciousness. Ramana Maharshi says our knowledge and identity of what we are is false. He describes our deeper inner Self as 'eternal,' which arises and returns to the same source.

So essentially they both say our experience of who we think we are, our experience of ourselves as separate individuals is incorrect and that we are part of everything.

We know there is more to us than just thoughts which seem to disturb the peace of our consciousness. After much searching and enquiry we find out about our self by our self, that there is no individual to the ego, that the ego we thought we were is just a bundle of thoughts. It is only when we experience we are not what we think we are that we begin to ask 'Who am I.'

Yoga Swami, a little known sage from Sri Lanka wrote profoundly and simply about acceptance:

We do not know

All is truth

There is not a single thing that is wrong

It was all accomplished long, long ago [13]

∞

Natural Feelings

We seem to have a hidden unwritten agreement with the establishment, authorities and institutions to be in control of our emotions and to behave like obedient domesticated citizens. It is as if we are over-programmed to obey society's orders instead of respecting and following our more natural wilder feelings.

Because of this we think we should be polite and have good manners all the time. We behave as if there is an expectation for us to be silent about our inner pain and be ashamed of showing our feelings of grief in public. We think we will make other people uncomfortable, embarrassed.

In 'The Wild Edge of Sorrow' Francis Weller writes:

"It is an act of protest that declares our refusal to live numb and small. There is something feral about grief, something essentially outside the ordained and sanctioned behaviours of our culture. Because of that, grief is necessary to the vitality of the soul. Contrary to our fears, grief is suffused with life force. It is riddled with energy, an acknowledgment of the erotic coupling with another soul, whether human, animal, plant or ecosystem. It is not a state of deadness or emotional flatness. Grief is alive, wild, untamed; it cannot be domesticated." {14}

We can also think we will look like we are in the middle of having a "nervous breakdown" or have a "mental illness," when nothing could be more wrong. Although grief can overwhelm us and even incapacitate us, grief is not an illness or a mental health disorder.

The misguided fear that grief can easily make us mentally ill, helps to programme us even more to be scared of showing the natural wildness of our feelings, especially of letting go. We are expected not to get 'out of control,' in front of others.

Our wilder emotions have been partly taken over and sanitised by following standardised religious services. Our language is full of phrases to stop us showing our feelings. 'Now dry those tears,' is a mantra we can probably all remember from adults trying to stop us showing our feelings.

Tissues are used by emotional police as weapons to stop tears and emotions escaping and becoming embarrassing or shameful.

At the slightest sign of revealing our emotions, we are told not to show any weakness, to 'man up, to 'crack on,' to 'soldier on' and 'to get on with the next task.' If we disobey we have to apologise in shame and weakness.

Yes, natural raw wild feelings usually are uncomfortable for others to witness but expressing them and sharing them is one of the most important healing ways our grief shows it is alive, moving and trying to progress to eventually finding acceptance. These feelings should never be shushed to stop others feeling uncomfortable or embarrassed.

∞

Free Expression and Expectations

It is as if grief wants to let us be individual and react in our own personal way, but society wants us to conform, to be just like every other person and behave as expected, so we do not cause any bother.

Although they may seem completely at odds with each other, our personal expression of the natural wild feelings of grief and society's detached attitude to this actually share the same aim.

Albert Einstein, Ramana Maharshi, Rumi, Lau Tzu and the Buddha show us that our biggest problem is the error in thinking we are separate individuals. Grief can show us the natural wild powerful nature of our feelings and give us the opportunity to express this in our own way.

But perhaps grief also gives us much more than this because grief shows us that our own way is the same as everyone else's own way, that we are all the same.

Experiencing what everyone else experiences lets us experience a universal consciousness which is common to all, irrespective of our culture or our religion.

∞

Grief Without a Funeral

Funerals help to reinforce the reality of loss. They are an opportunity to gather together with family and friends to express our feelings and thoughts and to receive support from each other.

They are also an opportunity to hear reflections of the person's life and hear and share memoires of what the person meant to others.

If a funeral takes place too quickly, loved ones can still be in an acute state of shock and feel so numb that the effects of the funeral on them are missed.

In a death where the body cannot be found, and there is no funeral the grief process is made much more difficult and it often comes to a halt. In situations like this, if the body is found and a funeral can take place, grief can progress once again. Even with no body, a funeral service can still help to move through grief.

We are hard wired to go through grief and not suppress it. Our feelings have a natural wildness which is healthy and needs to be allowed to be expressed. Even though they might make others uncomfortable, they need to be expressed because there is nothing more uncomfortable than having wild feelings.

We need to give our more feral emotions expression because not being expressed gives them more wildness and can have consequences.

If we can't express our emotions, they can be shut off, as if they have been dealt with. But instead of being worked through they can be relegated to the unconscious where, imprisoned they can unpredictably surface and can stop us getting through our grief and getting on with our life in more healthy ways.

If we don't work through our emotions, they can grow like a festering wound and cause us all sort of physical and psychological problems.

At a crematorium, a friend's wife screamed out his name as his coffin started to move along the rollers towards the curtain. She screamed his name out so loud and long. It was the most piercingly painful scream which cried out the pain of loss. Everyone stood still and you could hear them all take a big breath in because here they heard and felt the natural raw wildness of grief which they immediately identified with.

We should not be scared of the natural wild feelings of someone's grief. Instead we should do everything we can to encourage a person in grief to let their feelings have a voice.

We probably don't do this because we are scared we might encourage something to be 'un-boxed' which we can't 'box up' a gain. But this is just not the case as we are much better at regaining and maintaining our emotional equilibrium than losing it.

Unlike other cultures in the east, many western cultures have become more distanced and sheltered from close participation in funeral rituals. In India, the body is carried openly in public to the cremation ground. Family members not only prepare the body by washing it and dressing it but are present during the cremation. The oldest son lights the funeral pyre.

In the UK it has been possible for the last five years to avoid the funeral process altogether. There are now Direct Disposal' funerals which are unattended, without a service and without mourners present. Once the death certificate has been registered and the cremation form signed, the body is simply put on the next 'run' of cremations at the crematorium, which could all be completed the same day. Like many new ways of doing things, there can be positive and also negative aspects to not having a funeral.

Choosing not having a funeral creates a situation where we think we can separate our grief off and end it as soon as the body is removed from where the person died. We may even think we can avoid grief this way.

Some people may prefer to do this but for others the presence of mourners is essential to express their thoughts and feelings and get support with other people.

These are solemn opportunities to express our selves not only as individuals or as family members but also as friends in unique ways.

During the Covid-19 pandemic, deaths were frequently in isolation in hospital, so relatives could not be present. Other deaths were at home with greatly reduced access to all the usual care which reduced medical and nursing support.

Attendance at church services and funerals was strictly limited because of the risk of contracting Covid-19 which lead to a sharp increase in the use of Direct Disposal funerals. Wakes after funeral gatherings and commemorative services were all severely reduced or not allowed.

The unusual combination of family, social and community isolation regulations together with social distancing and Direct Disposal undoubtedly prevented further infections and deaths. But the downside was the absence of people able to be present to show their compassion, to express and share their grief. This all resulted in reduced support to help us go through the grief process.

Instead of watching someone being taken hostage by their grief, we can intervene by looking and listening to what is happening to them. We can see them more than once or twice. We can look at grief as something that needs much more time than we think it needs for expression. Instead of letting someone quietly grieve alone, we can make more of an effort to actively be with them.

Instead of grief taking someone as a hostage, we can help them grasp grief and use it to reshape them in a way which helps them keep moving with it and through it. We only have to be there. We only have to listen.

Some people have expectations about grief which assume that grief is a time limited experience after the death of a person someone loved. But this is not what most people experience.

When acceptance is beginning to be felt, it is not the ending of grief but a change in how we are living with the person who has left their body. It is the continuation of the other person with us in a new way.

∞

The Grip of Grief

When we see how others seem to have moved through their grief, we see that grief lessens its hold on them. We see they keep their treasured experiences and memories but have somehow let go of their old life and have changed, moving into a new life.

As grief lessens its hold on us, it gives us hope that our pain will eventually ease and we will be able to come out the other side of grief and have a new life and be happy again. But feeling some relief can make us feel guilty and disloyal for thinking about giving up our old life. This can make us feel more waves of the pain of loss.

Part of us wants to stay in the past with our old life but part of us wants to move into our new life, which sets up a struggle, like a tug of war. The tension can make us feel like we are frozen and can't move either way. It can be like a long dark winter with deep sadness and more suffering from the pain of loss. It can be helpful to ask what your loved one would say to you. It can also help if you ask what you would say to someone else in this position.

We do not understand what changes us and makes us slowly move. Perhaps we can't endure any more pain and suffering, so we are almost forced to make a choice to move to a different place with our treasured memories and experiences, to a place with less pain.

Although we might appear to move away from suffering to happiness, the scars of suffering become the foundation of happiness. Maybe like building a house, the suffering we have endured has slowly, but unknown to us, been forming the base on which we can build.

We see that our suffering has carried us through but perhaps we don't carry suffering, suffering carries us. Maybe suffering and happiness depend on each other for us to experience full consciousness.

This slow letting go of our old life and accepting what can be our new life, requires energy and effort in taking steps towards making a new life. For each step you take towards making a new life, your new life takes several steps towards you.

At this time we may start to be grateful to the person we have lost in new ways, realising they showed us certain things no one else did. We might see what they showed us about ourselves.

Grief gives us an opportunity to question and to re-vision what we see in our life. A place can be reached deep inside us where we can begin to see everything differently. In grief we can ask again 'Who am I?' in relation to the wider world, to everything and the whole Universe. It is an opportunity to see we are not isolated but along with the person we have lost, we can see our Self as part of everything.

Perhaps when we look outside we see the world but when we look inside we see the Universe. When we look at the day time sky we can see the bright blue sky, the sun, the moon and maybe some clouds. At night when we look at the sky, the sun is not seen but we can see more because we can see the stars and we know there is so much more we cannot see.

Although we are taught to think that time and space are real and even though this may be true, we know time and space are only ideas from thinking.

We are conscious there may be other planes of existence and levels of consciousness which we cannot see or understand because they are beyond thinking.

If we close our eyes and look inwards, we can see with our consciousness that we are not just an individual but part of everything in the Universe.

Albert Einstein, Ramana Maharshi, Rumi, Lau Tzu and the Buddha show us that our biggest problem is the error in thinking we are separate individuals. Perhaps it takes grief to show us we are not and to begin seeing ourselves as one.

References

1. https://www.webmd.com/heart-disease/can-you-die-broken-heart

2. https://biblehub.com/isaiah/61-1.htm

3. https://buddhiststories.wordpress.com

4. https://www.youtube.com/watch?v=FFyMG4mI_oQ

5. Sri Ramanasramam, Talks-With-Sri-Ramana Maharshi (1994)

6. Sri Ramanasramam, Talks With Sri Ramana Maharshi 1994. Talk 20 p.18

7. A Storr, Feet of Clay - A Study of Gurus (1996) Harper Collins, p 231.

8. Lau Tzu, Tao Te Ching Gia-Fu Feng and Jane English. (1989) Vintage, Chapter 56.

9. Sri Ramanasramam, Talks With Sri Ramana Maharshi, 1994. Talk 276 p.242-243

10. https://atkinsbookshelf.wordpress.com/2019/04/19/einsteins-touching-letter

11. Rumi. Fountain of Fire. Translated by Nader Khalili (1994) Cal-Earth Press

12. Victor Frankl, Mans Search for Meaning (2004) Rider p.84

13. Yogaswami, Natchintanai- (2004) Thiruvadi Trust p 3

14. Frances Weller, The Wild Edge of Sorrow (2015) North Atlantic Books p. 9.

[Written with Peter Egan, actor and animal advocate. First published as two parts in the 'Mountain Path' July 2022, Vol 59 No 3 and October 2022, Vol 59 No 4.

∞

2.

Cloghans

"He's gone," She said. There was a long pause.

I held the phone to my ear and felt the silence of the aftermath, the moment after the death announcement. This was immediately followed by a sense of solemnity.

My mind, frozen and numb in shock just let the body take over. A gnawing physical emptiness in my stomach appeared.

"We will be on the first plane over and see you later this afternoon," I said.

It was ten o'clock on a Saturday morning. My uncle had died just a few minutes before in hospital aged eighty two.

I went into the kitchen and told Chrisie my wife and India my daughter. We all said some things which are now forgotten. Life seemed to be put on hold and it all appeared hazy and blurred for a while.

I wanted some time on my own so I walked upstairs to be alone in the front bedroom overlooking the River Severn, looking west towards Ireland where he had been born and where he had also died. From the bedroom window I was looking out at the estuary of the River Severn, the large crack like an open mouth, between south Wales and England, probably visible from the Moon.

As I looked over the river going out to sea, I thought of

his spirit rising up, leaving Ireland, leaving this world. 'Goodbye, goodbye old friend, now to become an ancestor. Goodbye . . . forever.' There was a reluctance to cry, to let the tears come. It wasn't time.

Again, I felt the discomfort in my stomach. The pain reminded me of the loss which I had first felt just after my father died thirty years before, then last felt ten years ago when my mother died. But this wasn't so overwhelming. It was the same quality; just a lot less intense.

I stood looking out of the window into imagined faraway places down the river. Easily visible to the North across the Severn lay Wales, whilst England lay to the South.

The large bedroom window also overlooked the shutdown Berkeley Reactors 1 and 11 which stood up like window-less monoliths just half a mile away, having formed the first commercial nuclear power station in the world until they were shut down.

He had worked on them both with the construction company Taylor Woodrow as a senior electrical engineer in 1959. I thought how just like the power station, he too was now switched off.

Berkeley 1 and 11 had ceased operation in 1979 and he left to go back to Ireland in 1999 after a career as a civil engineer. He went back to retire and die and in 2008 he just had more than the ten years there he predicted.

As a boy he had won a scholarship to Nathy's boarding school in Ballaghaderreen in the west of Ireland but had contracted TB and had to return to live at home in his sixth form. So he didn't go to university; something which was unfortunate for him because he was particularly bright. He could quote Shakespeare and do calculus; the latter a subject which held no interest for me because I believed it was both beyond my grasp and well, not interesting to me. He then excelled at Gaelic football playing for his hometown and county. After school he left Ireland and spent all his time in England.

But eventually, like many people from the west of Ireland, he returned for his last decade to live close to what he saw as the motherland from which he came.

I had last seen him three months before. He was always a large man, blue eyes with silver hair swept back revealing a broad forehead. He was tall and broad with a very positive attitude. He was good natured with a twinkle in his eye. He had been through enough to always want to see the good in people. He had a soft spot for my daughter and my wife and we were fond of him.

Our parents were dead and because he was the last of that generation, we regarded him as the elder of the tribe, the person with insight and wisdom. He was my mother's older brother and had married in his forties. I knew him better than my three other Irish uncles and we got on well. One of us always had a glint in the eye about how good life could be. We were positive about life and always glad to hear from each other.

So just a few minutes after the call, the three of us had already psychologically left our home and we were heading to Ireland. An hour after the call we were at Birmingham Airport on the forty-five minute no frills budget flight to Knock Airport in county Sligo in the west of Ireland. The forty-five-minute hire car drive from Knock took us to be with Brendan's widow in Ballina in County Mayo.

Whatever you are doing after a death; for some days it seems you are really in a choiceless automatic state of mourning. It is almost like being hungry all the time but you can only be in that state and no other. People may come and go; so might you in that you go here and there but you are in that altered automatic state of consciousness . . . which does pass. It slowly diminishes when you start doing your normal duties again. That's how it was with me. I accepted that powerless feeling of being on automatic pilot.

The meeting and outpouring of empathy and compassion between bereaved ones can never be described in words, so I'll leave it there. But there was something very special to me that I will share with you that I had never experienced before and not even heard described; so I'll try and tell you as best as I can . . .

We returned to the funeral home in the evening and the body, what was left of Brendan, had been brought up from the hospital in Galway to the undertakers and had already been dressed and coffinised. There is s single moment of physical shock when you see someone you have always known, emotionally now cut off from them.

Brendan looked like his father had looked when he was dead. Horizontal, still and pale with a slightly Roman almost hooked nose. I'll probably look like that when I'm dead, I thought . . . if I don't die with traumatic wounds to the face. My thoughts went over the things I couldn't say to myself or to him.

Jim, my aunt's brother arrived. He had a two-inch-long dark brown beard and long dark brown hair. Jim listened carefully to the funeral director as he was given instructions for the gravediggers.

It seemed that because Brendan was a large man the funeral director was making sure that the grave was going to be big enough for the coffin.

"Tell the grave digger it's got to be three wide, eight long and five deep. Make sure now it's five feet. It has to be that. If it's for a double grave to include your sister here in the future, it must be at least five feet deep."

She didn't seem to mind being reminded of her own future death. But what is there to be surprised about; only that we are surprised by it when we shouldn't be.

"Got it. Five feet deep," Jim answered. I had never heard instructions given to someone to pass on to grave diggers before. But these were someone's last vital statistics and they had to be right.

"That's the crucial one to remember. Can't be taking his coffin out to dig deeper years later."

"Got it," repeated Jim. Jim had listened and repeated it to us as we walked out. "I've got it. Five feet deep," he said to his sister. As if it would help him remember the numbers to pass on to the grave digger. "Five feet deep," he said to me too, as if I should remember it in case he forgot it.

The next morning I felt like a week had passed. There were brief chats with people I knew and people I didn't know, at the house, on the way to the newsagent, on the phone and everywhere I went.

There were condolences warm wishes and remembrances from people about Brendan. But we had to get on with the business of moving towards the funeral and burial.

In the afternoon I had to go and meet Jim to check the gravediggers had the right measurements for the grave. The graveyard was several miles out of town and I assumed that because the grave diggers were independent of the funeral home, we had to double check they got the size of the grave right.

India had been particularly close to her great Uncle Brendan as she had never met any of her grandparents. Not knowing your grandparents is one of the problems children have when their parents are older than other parents; like me.

I was consciously and deliberately taking her to the graveyard because I thought visiting the site where he was going to be buried would soften the sight of seeing Brendan's coffin being taken from the church to the graveyard and being lowered into his grave. I thought it would help her move on. I also thought it would probably be good for me too.

For a child there is nothing worse than being treated like you don't actually know what is going on when you know full well what it is going on, and sometimes better than the adults.

On our way to the graveyard I remembered a young woman came to see me who had alcoholic parents. Her parents ignored the fact that her grandmother was seriously ill and actually dying. When she was thirteen, she spent all her spare time looking after her grandmother and just being with her.

When her grandmother became very unwell, the girl told

her alcoholic parents but they ignored her. She told them her grandmother needed to go to hospital but they ignored her so she called an ambulance and went to the hospital with her grandmother.

She called her parents to say her grandmother was dying but they just said she would be OK. She died after just a few hours. When she died, she was the only person with her.

After the funeral, when they all got back to the house, the girl was told to go outside and play in the garden whilst her parents and relatives ate and drank inside.

Now as a young woman, she needed to talk through her parent's behaviour but also, what she did, needed acknowledgement.

Because of hearing of experiences like this, I thought that if my daughter, who was only six years old, was more involved in her great uncle's funeral that she might cope better.

Brendan had mentioned a couple of times to me that he had a plot where he and his wife were going to be buried, but I hadn't really ever given it a second thought. But now I was driving along narrow Irish country lanes doing circles trying to find the plot in Cloghans graveyard which was apparently easy to find because it had an old run-down church in it. But with no-one about to ask the way, it was not easy to find. The name Cloghans has a silent 'g' and is slightly unusual, like the actual place itself.

I was told the old church was easy to spot as it had no roof, only the sides and gable end walls. But this did not seem to be my experience, perhaps because I just felt strange being in an area of Ballina I hadn't been to before. I followed several signs and eventually came to a building in the distance possibly fitting the description. Opposite the graveyard was the old church. I looked out for Jim, but couldn't see him.

In my bones I had the sense that even for the west of Ireland, this area was not just rural and isolated, but ancient with things around me I could not see, but which could perhaps sense me. It was an eerie area, not one I had sensed since I had stood with India and Chrisie on the shore of Iona four ears earlier.

I could hear and feel the wind. The view was stunning. In the distance was a large lake and above and behind it, a conical mountain like a volcano. It felt like the most still and serene place on earth.

The lake was Lough Conn, the seventh largest lake in Ireland. Brendan would have loved this place not just because the lake is connected to the Atlantic by the River Moy, but because The Moy was his favourite river, which he named his building business after, 'The Moy Construction Company,' or just 'The Moy' as he would refer to it as.

I parked the small hire car and India then walked into the graveyard, wandering around with me following her. She wandered around the graves happily whilst I wandered around looking at some of the epitaphs carved on the gravestones.

On a baby's gravestone I read "Those are not stars in the sky but portals though which our little ones watch over us." I thought of how much a child means to us and how much we mean to them. I thought about all my ancestors and I knew India was thinking about them too. I was happy for her to be wandering around the graveyard looking at the graves because I knew from my own childhood experiences of walking in cemeteries that they were a time of serenity and happiness for me.

I was wandering around the graves and was thrown back to when I used to walk back home from St Mary's Infant's school in Ipswich. I remember most the serenity of walking amongst the long dead. On winter afternoons I would walk down a long lane, alongside the outside wall of the graveyard as the gates were locked with chains and padlocks.

It was a thirty-minute walk and there was only one streetlamp at a grass triangle where the lane turned left down a hill leading to Tuddenham Road where streetlights re-appeared.

I remembered a gate at the bottom on the left which was locked in the winter. It was at the bottom of the hill and at the bottom of some steps. But the dark never scared me. I too was six or seven then. It was the old graveyard in Ipswich. During spring and summer afternoons on the way home from infants' school, when it was not so dark and spooky, the gates of the cemetery were open and then I walked on the path on the other side of the six foot high green metal fence, inside the graveyard, following the same route as the lane and the six foot high green metal fence.

At the end of the path were some steep winding steps leading down to the end of the lane and the gate was open. I remember thinking then that the steps were a way from the dead back to the living.

There was all the time in the world without any pressure, to look at all the weeds, wildflowers and lichen on all the old graves. Usually, I would go wandering and look at the names and the dates on the graves. It was something adults didn't talk about, so I was discovering the world of the dead for myself.

These people didn't try and tell me what to do, to control me or do me any harm. They weren't enemies or bad in any way. They were almost like friends, letting me just be. I came to see these walks by the cemetery as times of freedom and serenity.

It was freedom from school and home. The walks through

the graveyard were some of my peak moments as a child. It was how the world was to me then, a place of stillness and calm in the middle of a turbulent childhood. At either end of the graveyard were adults; at school giving instructions, commands, tasks and at the other end parents strained by their own turbulent childhoods. This was the first thing I had found to do to escape from them both sets of adults.

And now at the newly discovered Cloghans I still had the same sense. My six year old daughter was the same age I was then. I could not help wondering what was she thinking about being in a graveyard for the first time? She seemed happy and content, with not a care in the world which made me remember how I used to feel at that age.

We must have wandered around for twenty minutes looking at names and the ages of all those buried there then I heard the engine of a vehicle. I raised my head to see that it was a pick-up truck trying to get in the graveyard. The driver had got out to open the cemetery gates.

Looking in the distance, across two stone walls, I could see a large bright yellow digger which was used to dig the graves, but it seemed to be parked up and not in use. I walked with India over to the pick-up truck which was now purposefully driving across the graveyard towards us. When it stopped I recognised Jim.

"How ye?" he said, lowering the driver's window so he could lean his elbow on the open window frame. Jim looked a bit dishevelled, his hair everywhere a mess, like his clothes. It seemed to me that he had probably come straight from his farm because he had brought the pickup truck with his tools in the back. He had a friendly gentle smile.

"Good," I said. India smiled at him and I noticed there was a car behind him with Jonny, Brendan's other brother-in-law at the wheel. His son Declan who was maybe twenty sat beside him.

"Couldn't find the plot," I said.

"I'll show you. Follow me." So, we walked slowly beside the pick-up truck as it turned left and stopped halfway along the bottom row of graves. I noticed then that Cloghans was only about a quarter full as it had plenty of empty space for new graves. There could be at least another twenty rows I thought.

Jim got out of the pickup truck and I scratched my head as to why he had stopped here.

"Here," Jim said. Jonny and Declan had now got out of their car. I looked at them and at Jim as he looked head bowed looking at the ground. I must have looked bewildered because I felt it.

"Where's the plot?" I asked Jim, who looked up at my eyes for the answer. He was silent but he nodded to himself and looked down at the grass around our feet. There was no awkwardness just a solemn silence with respect for the grassy spot. Then Jim broke the strange silence and spoke first.

"If the first turf's not struck within two days, they say its bad luck and it'll soon be turned again. Let's measure it and get the turf off first."

"What do you mean?" I asked. Jim looked down at the ground in front of us.

"It's a belief that if you don't dig the grave within two days, someone else will die."

I noticed there was a pickaxe, a sledgehammer and other tools in the back of Jim's pick-up. I suddenly saw there were also several shovels and spades which made me feel the rush of adrenaline in my stomach followed by a slight race in my heart rate.

I was surprised by what I realised but not anxious or fearful in any way. My mind was open to what it was about to experience because there was no other way of dealing with my own and my young daughter's predicament.

There were no grave diggers. We were the grave diggers. We were going to dig the grave ourselves. The yellow digger in the distance was only for the locals who were too old to or who no longer went along with the tradition of digging the graves of your relatives. I looked beside me to see if India had realised what was happening.

"So, let's make a start," Jim said looking directly at me. As I bent down to whisper in India's ear.

"We are going to dig Uncle Brendan's grave," I said

"Yes, he will be so happy." Her answer surprised me and made me realise how completely normal it must be for a child to think the family should perform the last duties such as digging the hole in the ground for the body; but as a society we do not.

We have accepted the programming that we should distance ourselves from any close contact with most of the aspects of the dead. We have become observers attending a funeral, not participants in our final ritual and have given up part of the grieving process.

We were about to experience physically and emotionally all of the forgotten realities of digging a grave for someone you love.

I remembered seeing a man who had chronic difficulty maintaining relationships with women. He appeared to find it difficult to speak about his mother and to connect with any feelings about her. He had a sadness about him which he talked about with frustration and tears.

He had been kept away from every aspect of his mother's death. The only thing he could remember about the death of his mother was when he heard it announced from the church pulpit on a Sunday morning. He wasn't allowed to go to the funeral and he wasn't even told where his mother was buried.

He acknowledged that he had never had a chance to say goodbye to his mother and he felt blocked and confused about her. Eventually he came up with and talked through his plans which involved finding out where his mother's grave was. He then planned to have his own ceremony there to say goodbye to her.

On the day he chose to find her grave, he dressed in his best clothes and went to the graveyard alone. He took a letter he wrote which he read out aloud to her over her grave. It was a long letter saying everything he had missed saying to her as her son who was left behind. He planted some daffodil bulbs and then had some picnic food he had prepared.

Before he left the grave, he set off some fireworks. When I saw him a few a weeks after, his sadness had gone. He had a lightness in his face and in his eyes. He had completed his part in his mother's funeral and worked through his unexpressed grief.

Even when we have no way of going back in time and compensating for lost opportunities to grieve, this young man's story shows that we can create our own personal way of going through our grief.

The five of us, Jim, Jonny, Declan, India and I stood there for a few seconds looking down at the imaginary boundary of the grave plot.

"Eight by three, by five," Jim said as he measured out eight feet by three feet with a simple tape measure. He marked off the four corners with four tent pegs and one piece of string.

I was in a state of bewilderment because these were the instructions Jim wanted me to remember, I had never seen a grave dug before. I had also never dug a grave and my daughter was going to dig our uncles grave right now.

"Here take this spade," Jonny said, handing me a spade from the truck. He turned around then grabbed three shovels from the truck to give to me.

With my hands full I ended up giving one to India which she passed on to Declan, who put it down on the grass. India held on to her shovel. We looked at each other. We were all now a family team with a single job to get done together; to dig Brendan's grave.

Then Jim started clearing the rubbish off the grass, scraping it with the front of the spade. His spade stopped at something which I bent over and picked up.

"It's a flat squashed tin of lager. Looks like it's been run over by a steam roller,' I said.

"Well, well," Jim said as he took it from me and laughed. "

"He was more of a Guinness man," Jonny added. Everyone laughed and it was the release of tension through dark humour which we all needed to actually begin, get stuck in and start digging Brendan's grave.

I had been bewildered by everything so far and I must have seemed as if I was in a daze. I couldn't find any comfort zone, or anywhere in me which felt normal about digging Brendan's grave because this was not usual for me.

But it was normal on some deep level I knew was good and the right thing to be doing. I only felt strange because it was entirely new.

No one had actually talked about digging Brendan's grave or hinted at it or used any euphemism. Perhaps digging your loved one's graves was respected and viewed as being too solemn to be given any words.

I could only remember very vaguely as a child hearing about how some old families in the west of Ireland dug the graves themselves and buried their own. My aunt's family was one such family and my mother's family had also done this a long time ago.

We were all doing this right now. Digging the graves of your family is an ancient practice of the people of the extreme west of Ireland. There had been no chatter or idle talk about it. It was approached in a reverent silence with respect for the dead . . . to a point.

I knew India would be coping much better with digging her great Uncle Brendan's grave because she knew no different. But when I reconsidered this, I thought that she would find it odd as well because no-one had ever mentioned digging a grave to her. But there again why should a child find another new thing in their lives any more surprising than any of the other new things they come across.

I had never met anyone who had ever dug a grave and still haven't.

"Are you OK? I mean OK about digging Brendan's grave?"

"Yes." She beamed a happy smile to me which told me she was good with it all.

I wandered several times around the outskirts of the very shallow hole left by the absent turf. India helped to clear the little bit of turf which Jim had managed to dig up. The turf was about three to four inches thick.

She was completely absorbed in what she was doing and

what she was part of.

India, Jonny and Declan similarly busied themselves with dealing with the turf skimmed from the top of the grave plot. Within 10 minutes it looked like a very good shallow outline for a grave with a foot high mound of turf piled up at the head end. As Jim seemed to be the person who knew most about what we were all doing, if not the only person who knew what we were doing, I thought I would ask him about what we were actually doing.

"Do many families dig the graves like this?" I asked.

"Not so many these days. Maybe one in ten I guess." Apart from being a farmer, Jim was also the singer and mandolin player in a local band. He was a fit man and had the most stamina of all of us.

"Have you done this many times?"

"Eleven now," he said starting to break the earth. I could see beads of sweat breaking out on his forehead.

"Here let me have a dig." I took the spade and proceeded to dig into the earth.

At first the earth was cold, damp and heavy, but it quickly seemed to have changed. I noticed it began to have a warmth to it just like good cloth does. It was the final thing which would cover Brendan. It was like I was preparing his clothes. It became a warm thing to be doing, not a cold exercise of shovelling earth. Just as an expectant parent prepares a crib to welcome the new-born baby, so I was preparing the earth to welcome Brendan back.

This sense of welcoming extended to the mountain, the lake, to the rest of Ireland, the sky and the sea. I had never experienced this before and I wondered if it was because I was actually in the grave, with the soil, aware of how it can envelope us that I had this new sense of its importance.

Here the live earth welcoming back its own was nakedly real.

I noticed there were a few stones, but not too heavy for the spade to lift up. I dug with the spade for about five minutes and when there was so much loose earth that there was nowhere else for me to stand but for me to stand on it and compress it, I switched to the shovel to lift the loose earth out of the grave.

Twenty shovels later and the beads of sweat from my own forehead had formed thick drops of sweat which fell onto the lenses of my glasses. I had trouble seeing through the blurred sweat covered lenses. I wiped them with my shirt and saw India watching Jim and Jonny and Declan looking at me.

At first, I had appeared fit and strong but now I was just at the end of my strength. Five more shovels and even when I wiped my glasses, I couldn't see through the blurriness of the sweat on my lenses because now they were also misting from the heat from my head. So, I had to stop. But I stopped mainly because I was exhausted.

India was handing mints around which Jonny had given her and she was eating them like they would all be soon gone. I felt and saw Jim use a bottle to tap the side of my upper arm which was holding the shovel.

"Have a drink," he said.

"Couldn't think of a better drink," I said drinking a mouthful. The ice-cold liquid hit my tongue, the inside of my cheeks, the roof of my mouth and when the coolness hit my gullet, then my stomach, it jolted me into full consciousness. I gulped down three more mouthfuls and felt my thirst was quenched and the sugar entering my blood stream. I felt a little dizzy from the rush of the sudden entry of water and sugar into my system.

We all stood and passed around the bottle in a social moment where it was time to share any words we had in our hearts or minds.

"When I dug the first couple of graves, we didn't have bottles of lemonade. My uncles and brothers had bottles of whisky and by the end of it, if you hadn't actually fallen into the grave; you were ready to lay in the grave and go to sleep," Jim said, smiling and taking a good look at the state of me, already soiled with the earth.

"I feel like that already," I said. As I wiped fresh soil off the bottom of my trouser legs.

Then, out of nowhere, I felt a stillness standing in the middle of all of these graves. Here with my family the stillness reminded me of the stillness I felt on those walks through the graveyard in Ipswich when I was six or seven. There was silence as everyone rested and there was a great peace within me. It felt like it was for a few minutes or maybe it was the stillness always here inside me.

"It's a lot more work than you would think," Jim said. I was proud of the work I had done as I had managed to take Jim's four inches of turf down by about nine inches; so, we had done one foot in half an hour.

"So how long do you think it will take us to do the next four feet?" I enthusiastically and rather confidently asked Jim; thinking he would say maybe an hour to an hour and a half.

"Four to five hours if we are lucky"

"You've got to be kidding. Are you serious?"

"It'll take that long at least."

"Why four to five hours. I mean we lifted out a foot

in half an hour."

"What you've been up to so far shovelling is the easy layer on the top compared with the rest."

"I'm interested now."

"Well, the rest comes with ever increasing pain. When you are in a hole four feet deep there are two sources of massive effort." Jim looked at the others then at me.

We all went quiet as Jim began to dig. After fifteen minutes he handed the spade over to me. But after only ten minutes digging, I handed it over to Jonny and I then had a rest for five minutes.

I was standing in the grave where Brendan's feet would rest in the coffin. I stood silent but I felt I was almost thinking aloud . . . 'So, this is where he will end up for eternity or until the world goes dark as the sun goes out or it is destroyed by a comet or whatever.'

"Odd to think this is where he will be forever,' Jim said, almost reading my mind.

"Yes, for all time. Maybe thousands of years," I replied.

"But he would have chosen this spot because it

looks over the lake to the mountain."

"Yes, it must have seemed so special."

"Some say the best spot in the West."

"It's strange that we spend a lot of time getting everything ready for a new born baby to arrive into a happy home. We spend a lot of time helping someone to get ready to be married but we don't do much for when someone dies apart from make arrangements. This is so different. It is complete involvement; complete immersion, literally in the actual ground."

"A great reminder of our own short time here too," Jim added.

I noticed we were all doing a lot of looking down at the ground then looking up at the sky. It was as if each of us was trying to work something out, reconcile something, and see some link between the earth and the heavens.

I noticed we each did it in an almost compulsive way every once in a while. It was a new body language as if we had to emotionally compensate for the immersion in the feminine mother earth. There was an acceptance of her welcoming back the return of one of her own.

But maybe this intense immersion, actually in the earth, needed to be compensated for by looking at the opposite;

the great spirit of the sky. Perhaps this body language I saw was simply about restoring inner balance in this traditional ritual.

When I got my breath back from all the talking and thinking, I realised I had been standing for a while looking at the mountain. I used the shovel to move the earth which we had all shifted away from the edge of the grave. Jonny handed the spade over to Declan. Declan was the fittest and dug for fifteen minutes.

Finally, India was given the spade and also dug. She dug with the same enthusiasm as everyone, digging and carefully lifting earth out of the grave.

This went on in cycles of passing the spade and shovels around in a very well organised manner. But we slowed down as the hole got deeper and had breaks every fifteen minutes for lemonade and mints.

Eventually curiosity as to why Jim was so sure about his four to five hour estimate got the better of me.

"There can't be any big surprises," I said.

"See that long handled shovel." Jim pointed to the tools on the ground. "The handle is six foot long and it only has a small shovel blade so that when you are in a four foot deep hole, you can still lift it up above your head. You have to lift it up two feet above your head to seven or eight feet from the bottom of the hole to get the dirt out. You can only lift a little at a time."

"Yes, I can see now just how that can get more difficult. So, what's the second source of massive effort?"

"That." Jim first pointed to the mountain in the distance, then to the sledgehammer.

"I don't get it. The mountain and the sledgehammer. What do you mean?"

"We have a lot of that mountain in here." Pointing to the mountain again, "And we have to use that," pointing down to the sledgehammer.

Jim handed me the spade again as it was probably my third time to dig but when I dug, I was stopped abruptly by a solid mass of something.

Jim heard the noise, saw my face and pointed to the mountain again. Now I knew what he meant.

"Granite. Solid granite boulders."

"How do you know?

"I've dug in this graveyard and it's the same every time. You are OK for the first three feet then you hit this layer of boulders which cover the whole of the ground at that level. It looks like an hour and a half job getting the soil out but you can't lift these boulders out. You have to break them up with a sledgehammer. You'll see."

The cycles of digging continued around the boulder which was in the centre of the plot at about three and a half feet. Another one appeared at the foot of the plot and then another at the side of the plot. The one in the right hand side wall of the grave eased out with some effort, fell on the floor, then couldn't be moved.

So, we had about a foot and a half of dirt to clear and three boulders which we couldn't even move. This is where the pickaxe came into its own.

We dug around them and under them and got down on our hands and knees to clear as much soil as possible and then the tough work started. We didn't even try to lift them out.

We stopped for another rest, leaning on shovels and pickaxes.

Jim picked up the sledgehammer and leant on its thick handle.

"Lincoln was a grave digger," Jim said.

"Abraham Lincoln?" I asked.

"Yes, he was a sexton in a church in Indiana. You know someone who looks after the buildings and the land including the graves."

"Never knew that," I said.

"Tall too. Six foot three. When he was shot, he was taken to a house across the road from the theatre in a coma. He was too tall for the bed, so he had to lie diagonally. Lay like that for nine hours in a coma before he died. Grave robbers tried to steal his body for a ransom but they got caught.

They opened his grave in 1901 and took a photo of him. You never know when you are last going to be disturbed but no one's going to be interested in the likes of us. We will lay in peace. I'll bet Lincoln never had to use a sledgehammer in the graves he dug."

Jim went silent as he started chipping away at one of the big rocks which was two foot long and a foot wide. After ten minutes he handed me the sledgehammer.

"Five minutes is all I can do," I said, once more with sweat pouring off my forehead and down the lenses of my glasses. "I feel like a convict breaking rocks" I added. But five minutes was the same for each of us with an extra heavy sledgehammer.

It was as much as any of us could do. Only one of every

five hits at a granite stone would yield a chip off the stone. So, it was painfully slow, as Jim said and it began to feel like we could not break the rocks up and complete our task even in five hours.

"Now. Let's get rid of the rocks," Jim said. It was an announcement that the boulders were finally broken up small enough for us to carry.

I looked at India who had also had a short period of trying to break up rocks and she still looked happy to be in and around the grave helping with everything as part of the family team.

"All pieces of stone have to be lifted out of the hole, put on the side and then we get rid of them. When we start the next dig, we don't want to have to lift all the stone out again. We'll carry them over to the stone wall over there and dump them over the other side."

Down at the end of the slope where future rows of graves would be dug was the stone wall. No carrying device was available so we each cupped our hands full of bits of broken of rock.

After forty minutes of removing the broken up bits of rock, the biggest chunk of broken rock had to somehow be lifted out. It could only be lifted by three men. It had to be lifted four feet up to the edge of the hole which was now nearly a grave.

Once out it was easy to move and Jonny and Declan then rolled it down the gentle slope with their feet to the three foot high stone wall. They then they lifted it over the wall, dropped it on the newly broken pieces of stone and the small heaps of dead flowers from recent funerals.

"We need to straighten up the walls a bit," Jim said.

"You've got a keen eye, so give it a go." Jim continued looking at me with a questioning expression.

"I'll give it a go," I said kneeling down before sitting on my bottom then sliding down into the grave.

The grave was deep now, I thought. Since my last turn of digging, the others had flattened the bottom out at about five feet. My mind started to wander . . . 'I've never been in a grave before and the next one I will probably be in will most likely be my own; if I am buried.'

I wanted to complete the task but I also wanted to get out of the grave because well, it was not mine. Graves are a place you don't want to be. It is a taboo like being in someone's secret place without them knowing. I hope you are happy here Brendan, I thought. Peace at last. No more work.

I used the larger shovel to scrape off earth from the sides, so the walls were more vertical but I was alarmed at just how much new earth I was filling up the grave with as it was going to be really hard work to lift it up at least seven feet with the long shovel. My mind went back to the most recent tomb I had visited in The Orkney . . . the Tomb of the Eagles.

The tomb which is over 5,000 years old and under ten metres long has to be entered by lying on a trolley on four wheels, which was like a large, modified skateboard. You have to lie on your back and pull the trolley along by a rope which is attached to the ceiling of the tunnel lined by massive stones. Pulling yourself on a trolley by a rope makes you realize that the only reason you can't just climb through is because the walls are several metres thick.

In the Tomb of the Eagles they found the remains of 342 people. It is believed that the bodies were left on slabs of stone at the entrance to the tomb, and when they had been picked bare by white tailed sea eagles, they were then interred further inside the tomb. I wonder if this allowed grieving time. Essentially, a body was put out of sight when the person was no longer in living memory. They had changed from relatives to ancestors.

Perhaps it was their way of coping with the loss of loved ones. I thought how digging this grave was allowing us to move on with the grief process.

Then I realised I was thinking about all of this whilst I still digging, so I stopped for a moment.

"Shall I keep going Jim?"

"Yes. It needs to be a little broader at the bottom, so it's squared all the way down. Don't worry about the earth. There are enough of us to get it all out."

"I was feeling a bit guilty about that."

"Don't worry. It's the easy bit now. It will make it look all square."

"Right then." I attacked the wall for the last time with the shovel and did the finesse work on the top bottom and sides.

"Can I help Daddy?" India said loudly.

"Of course. Hop in." I was surprised she wanted to join me in the grave but she probably heard this was the part that made it look good.

"It's nearly done isn't it?" She smile.

"Yes, nearly there."

"It's the last bit like icing a cake."

"Yes. I suppose it is." India had given me a sense that this ritual task was coming to a close. I knew I would probably never do this again. I scrambled up the sides of

69

the corner of the foot of the grave and sat on the corner looking at India. She was busy digging.

"Look daddy look daddy look!" she said. "Look, daddy. Gold!" I looked down and saw she had picked up a small rock about two inches wide by three inches long. It was glistening.

I thought I was seeing things for a moment.

"It's gold. Gold!" India said. I looked at her and her face was smiling brilliantly. "Gold," she said. I looked over to Jim who was smiling.

"It's gold alright," Jim said

"Gold, gold," India said even more excited

"Fool's gold," Jim said.

"Why is called Fools gold?" India asked.

"It's named that way because it's actually a type of silica, like the stuff sand is made of."

"Oh," said India disappointed. "I would have had to put it back to be with Brendan even it was real gold," she added. "It's not mine anyway . . . it's the Earth's." I thought about this for a while.

Just like the fool's gold is the earths, so is Brendan. And so are we. We all have to be returned to where we came from. We only leave what we have shown others about ourselves.

I was left thinking about memories we leave in other people's minds and ones which vanish with us and my thinking wandered off looking at this.

I thought of my uncle and what he would say about the shining Fool's gold and how he would smile at this with a twinkle in his eye .

Trying to remember how he looked made remember my favourite poem by Leonard Cohen about a woman called Anne . . .

For Anne

With Annie gone,
whose eyes to compare
with the morning sun?

Not that I did compare,
But I do compare
Now that she's gone.

When my mind had stopped wandering, I came back to the present . . . It now looks like a grave. It is a grave, I thought.

This is the interior of Brendan's grave. It's a good grave. Not just a hole. But a hole made with care and some precision to welcome his coffin.

Others will dig this out again to bury his wife. They won't have such a hard job as us breaking up and lifting all those rocks out. They will hit the top of his coffin with their spade and stop dead in the realisation that it's his coffin. Will I be there? Will any of us who are here now be there? I noticed India looking happy at her work smoothing the ground, the part where his head would rest.

"Great work," I said

"I'm making a comfy pillow for his head." She stood back and paused, looking at her work. Then she looked up at me. "Done Daddy."

"I'll lift you up and out,' I said and I jumped into the grave and knelt down. India climbed onto my knee then used my shoulder to lift herself up over the edge and onto the ground above the grave. Jim held her hand and steadied her as she stood upright. I carried on smoothing the floor of the foot of the grave. I didn't notice India being lowered down by Jim and re-joining me.

I was thinking to myself, 'A grave is the place a person stays the longest. The longest lasting structure they will be in.'

There's been no solemnity, I thought. No one has been

sad, miserable or morbid. It's been a strange task the main aim to make a good grave for Brendan. If anyone has any guilt bothering them when a person dies, then digging their grave would probably completely absolve them of it. I have no guilt looking back at my time with Brendan. I thought of my mother and their three brothers. Brendan was the last of that family.

I was jolted out of my dissociated state by a gentle slap on the back.

"Ok, you're done," said Jim.

I had been standing in the grave with a thousand-yard stare thinking to myself with India smoothing out the floor of the grave in what seemed like loving small strokes. This was wonderful closure for her but also for me. It had given us special almost sacred time that cannot be had elsewhere or in any other way.

After four hours the lemonade ran out and so did the mints. Both had been a good source of energy. Four and a half hours after we had cut the turf the grave was ready.

We were exhausted, covered in soil with wet clothes due to the perspiration.

"Here, give us your hand,' Jim said.

"Ok," I said, feeling my feet on the bottom of this

grave for the last time. I leant back against the wall behind me and put my right foot in the wall in front and leapt forwards and upwards as Jim's arm lifted me up in one powerful joint manoeuvre.

As I stood there Brendan now seemed like he was already a long way out to sea just as if he were in a burning Viking funeral boat which was about to disappear over the horizon.

There was now a perfectly symmetrical rectangular hole, eight by three by five feet with mostly flat walls and a flat bottom. There was a large mound of earth to the left which looked as if it came from three holes this size. Jim said that this could be shovelled back in fifteen minutes.

Half an hour later we were back at my aunt's house where she greeted us smiling.

"All done," India said. India was proudly smiling.

"You're both covered in soil. Did the two of you help?" she asked

"Help. The two of them dug at least half of it," Jim said.

"And you too India?"

"Yes. It's a really nice grave." My aunt had a happy

smile for India. She walked over to her and hugged her.

"You are such an angel. He would be so proud of you."

The next thing to do was to get cleaned up and then go straight away to the funeral home to meet and greet everyone who came to pay their respects to Brendan in his coffin. This was the modern version of a wake.

I found myself thinking about how modern man now has a form of body disposal known as direct commitment or more simply 'direct disposal.' Once the death certificate and cremation form are signed by doctors, the body is taken straight to a crematorium for disposal.

There is no service and no mourners. No feelings, no tears, no wildness. No sharing, no touching, no talking, no earth, no sky.

I sat with my aunt, Chrisie and India in a row of chairs facing the coffin which was open. The door opened at six and nonstop until eight o'clock, people briefly paused in front of us shaking all our hands, saying what were their last words about him.

Most seemed dressed in their Sunday best but some had come in straight from their farms, from manual work and were in their working clothes. I didn't count the hundreds of hands we shook because after the first hundred handshakes, all concentration was lost apart from being polite, solemn and maintaining eye to eye contact.

I heard many things said. Not the same thing was said to any of us. Each one treated us differently. Most went up to the coffin first, leant over and kissed his hands and said something quietly to him. Some kissed his forehead. The last of hundreds of people went through the doors two hours after we started shaking their hands.

There were a few lovely humorous things said and some very serious religious things as well. But everyone wanted to comfort us in their own personal way.

They were showing us we were part of a community, a family, which was their family. I must have seemed strange to everyone because I felt dissociated from what was going on. Yesterday morning we had all been at home. Now India and I had dug his grave and here we were with Chrisie and my aunt and Brendan for the last time, now prepared for the next day.

I wondered if he had any regrets. Then I thought would I have any and my mind wandered . . . I was making my own list of last regrets and trying to let go of them.

The next day we stood waiting outside the funeral home for the body to be placed in the hearse. We were to make the three minute walk behind the slowly moving hearse across the River Moy to Ballina Cathedral for the funeral service.

As soon as the hearse started moving, my aunt, Chrisie, India and myself were about to take the first step as the main family group behind the hearse when suddenly, India let out the most distressing cry of grief I have ever heard. It had such huge emotional power that everyone stopped for the three or four seconds until she had finished. Most including me had never heard such a shrill of such emotional power from someone's heart.

A few minutes later we walked into Ballina Cathedral and we took our family seats at the front. The organ filled the air with sweet sombre music as the coffin was carried slowly up the isle to the altar. As my uncle passed me by in his coffin, tears began to flow and I could not even see the coffin. But then my eyes dried and I could see clearly for the first time in a long while.

∞

One year later. After a night staying at a friend's house on the lower slopes of Crough Patrick, Ireland's most sacred mountain, we decided that on our last few days in the west of Ireland we would go and visit Uncle Brendan's grave in Cloghans cemetery.

It was suggested we go to an early morning gathering of

families there before dawn. We were not alone because there was for the third year a gathering in the abandoned church before dawn at six o'clock, which has carried on and so had become a new tradition.

We were not strangers to this graveyard because only recently, in terms of the age of the burial site we had dug his grave with other relatives.

But it was now so early in the morning and therefore too dark to see anything else other than the shadows of stone walls on the sides of the road. But above was the dark pre-dawn sky, brightly lit up with hundreds of thousands of stars.

The stars here reminded me of the epitaph only a short distance from where we stood, 'Those are not stars in the sky but portals through which our little ones watch over us.'

The abandoned church whose roof was the stars a floor made of a path of pebbles and neatly cut turf was now like a preserved monument. It held at least two hundred people in the pre-dawn of Easter Sunday.

I couldn't help ignoring what the priest said because he seemed almost irrelevant in the setting. You only need words to describe the ancient primal setting it if you are not there and only scripture to remind you if you have forgotten or lost touch with who you are and why you are there.

We were a community under the stars and had come to be with our ancestors, knowing our time would come only too soon.

No representative of any world religion could say better in words what we already sensed as true inside us, standing waiting for night to pass and dawn to arrive. There was a sense of the limited number of sunrises we would see and I noticed most of the people there were in awe waiting for the sun to appear.

As I stood there in the slowly emerging light of dawn, two sounds brought my mind to a halt and I stood totally humbled.

First it was the birds. Out of nowhere, a single bird suddenly began tweeting, then another and then more. Some began almost whistling and then singing in a full chorus as if to rejoice the day and expectation of the sun. The singing increased every few seconds.

Everyone listened for about a minute when they were interrupted by another sound. Their silence.

The birds suddenly stopped singing to listen to another sweet sound. They chose to stop to what they must have realised was for this moment, more important.

A teenage girl in an anorak, who was probably only thirteen years old, started playing a penny whistle perfectly. Suddenly there was silence. All the birds had stopped singing and stayed silent to listen to her for two minutes. The young girl could be seen though everyone's visible breath in the icy cold air.

Here was a simple communal consciousness uniting man with nature. It was under the faint light from the rising sun, only just beginning to dim the light from the stars.

It seemed like a reminder of the change that had taken place for those who had already been absorbed back into the earth. This was true ancestor worship.

When the young girl stopped playing the penny whistle, the birds immediately erupted into even louder song than before. Here with the faint rays from the sun taking over from the stars, no priest was needed as a master of ceremonies when hundreds of birds punctuated reality so spectacularly. Any remaining sense of the necessity of a religious priest were extinguished.

Any power or significance from religious words, gestures or symbols were totally eclipsed by the birds stopping singing to patiently listen to the girl playing a penny whistle, before the birds once again took their turn to sing, welcoming in the light and consciousness of another day on Earth.

This was significant. This was power. The finely tuned power of the meek.

The bird's singling gradually reduced as they flew off in small groups to begin their daily life which signally us to also leave. Family by family we slowly and silently walked out on to the road and through the gates of Cloghans to be at our family graves.

The rays of light from the early morning sun revealed the landscape I had forgotten. The graveyard faced the lake and on the other side of it was the granite mountain, now with its peak covered in snow thinning and fading further down its slopes. I remembered it well from digging my uncle's grave with my daughter who was now busy walking ahead of me, leading the way, looking for his grave.

Unlike the church which had been abandoned generations ago, the graves were not without human touch and care.

Religion had been repositioned in Ireland since I was a boy visiting there but this modern ritual showed that ancestor worship still guides many.

Because of the irreversible loss of its moral authority due to its scandal of secretly supporting corrupt criminal priests and nuns, the roofs would begin to fall in on other churches and temples around the world.

Imagining places like churches, temples, and schools which had their darker elements exposed and removed reminded me of the stripping back that is needed to see clearly.

Removal of our own veils of ignorance so we can be fully conscious made me remember a poem I had scribbled down . . .

Scriptures no longer needed

The Buddhas, the crucifixes,

The Natarajans have gone

The incense the candles,

The beads and the gong.

The Quran the Sutras,

The Bible's gone too.

With no Tanakh or Vedas,

All that's left is you.

What I had just seen in a previously deeply religious community was the gathering from our past the things we could practically use now. There was music from a child, from birds. There was the harshness of the change of a dark sky of twinkling stars to an early morning sunrise. There were friends and neighbours from the same community and also from far away.

Everyone had made a big effort to get there to be on time together. There was the communal ground, the motherland where everyone came from.

As my ability to see the stars above began to fade, I almost felt like saying to them, 'Don't go,' but that was replaced by a consciousness of what seemed like eternal union with them.

It was a feeling of peace, of happiness. It seemed the stars were not just looking down on us but were as much part of this, of us, of me, of the girl, the birds and our buried relatives, giving us a sense of all of this, of each of us being one thing, a consciousness of the unity of everything in the Universe.

The fading of the light from the stars reminded me that although for most of the day we cannot see them, the stars are as much there as they are at night. They are there day and night but not seen, like so many other things about ourselves which are there but we cannot see, sometimes simply because we do not take special time to look and see them. We can look at the Universe as consisting of all space, all of time, all matter, and energy, the planets, stars and galaxies. Or we can look at the Universe containing many other parallel Universes, the Multiverse.

The Multiverse, first described by the ancient Greeks, includes all space, all of time, all matter, and energy, the planets, stars and galaxies, other parallel Universes, all consciousness, everything known and unknown.

This is what I see when I think of the Universe as Everything. There is no reason to suppose that the ancient Greeks saw this any differently.

I realised what I witnessed was not just a new local form of post Christian Neo Pagan ancestor worship. It was so much more. It was practical expression of looking for and finding happiness which we know is deep inside us but we have difficulty accessing most of the time.

At an unusual time at the interfaces between day and night, between the mountain and the sky, between the sky and the water, we were gathering at the place which is the last home of our relatives, we were once again with them, reflecting on our own choices in life and seeing our own potential for wholeness and happiness.

A part of me wondered about this and I became concerned as I looked to the mountain in the distance because I imagined seeing a difficult future ahead.

I was not sure if I was just looking at my own personal experience or if my experience was a warning of a future where we might once again have to do very basic things such as make the coffins and dig the graves for our loved ones.

I was aware that my thoughts were trying to interrupt my consciousness of the happiness and stillness I was experiencing and once again I remembered what the little known obscure Sri Lankan Yoga Swami had said . . .

We do not know

All is truth

There is not a single thing that is wrong

It was all accomplished long, long ago

Remembering these words, I stopped fretting and there was serenity inside and outside of me of oneness with everything.

I stood looking at the slowly increasing light with no thoughts, just inner stillness. There were no words for the peace and happiness of this stillness. I was just this consciousness which was in everyone and everything around me, below in the ground and above in the stars. I felt at one with the Universe and immensely privileged to be here, conscious of what is right now, this present moment. Time seemed to be still too.

This state of just consciousness of a shared sense of oneness with everything comes with a mind not full of thoughts but full of stillness.

The whole place, time and timing had this effect on me as well as the presence of my family, living and gone.

I didn't go with any thoughts of why I felt like this, I just remained happy experiencing these precious moments. There were no reasons why I felt like this which could make me feel any better than I felt already.

During my childhood in Ireland, we were firmly told to be still during the Angelus which occurred three times a day. It was a simple remembrance to be still and conscious of this oneness.

As a teenager I of course rebelled against instructions and orders but now I fully understood the utter simplicity of the Angeles standing in the dawn next to what looked like an abandoned church.

The importance of the Angelus is not about remembering the dead. It's importance is about remembering ourselves, remembering to be conscious or our happiness.

This needs a little explanation.

∞

3.

Remember to Be Still

Happiness and Meaning

For millennia we have known how important happiness is because we know it is everyone's main desire and aim in life. One of the first people to have said this was the Greek philosopher Aristotle who in 300 BC wrote,

'Happiness is the meaning and purpose of life, the whole aim and end of human existence.' [1]

Although we have this information, because of distractions it seems we need to be frequently reminded of it. The need to remember that happiness is our main aim and purpose requires us to reset our default from 'thinking' back to our natural state of 'just being' happy.

There are many reminders to help us to attend to our inner self and be happy. Some are from the arts; few are direct whilst many are from religion. I remember during my childhood summer stays in the west or Ireland, each day being punctuated by a ritualistic Christian tradition of the ringing of bells to stop and be still, The Angelus.

The Angelus

The Angelus is a period of reflection three times a day which is announced by the tolling of a bell three times which is repeated three times, so that nine rings are heard.

Today, the bells still ring out at 6.00am, noon and 6.00pm. Everyone is expected to stop what they are doing, be still, look inwards and contemplate the Divine or pray.

It is reported that animals would automatically stop ploughing and stand still at the sound of the Angelus bell.

The Angelus originated in Italy in the 11th century and is still broadcast every day on Irish radio at 12.00 noon and at 6.00 pm and on Irish television every evening.

It is also broadcast every day on the radio stations in North and South America, Canada, Mexico and the Philippines.

Meditation

A relief sculpture estimated to have been carved around 2350 BC, could be the first recorded reminder for others to be happy.

The Pashupati Seal [2] is a soapstone seal discovered at the archaeological site of the Indus Valley Civilisation. It is thought to be the earliest prototype of the God Shiva. The seal shows a seated cross-legged figure in the yogic 'padmasama' or lotus meditation posture with arms pointing downwards.

It is important because it is one of the first communications from our ancient ancestors which reflects the stillness of looking inwards. That is having a still mind from having no thoughts.

A modern direct reminder is 'Attend to the purpose for which you have come,' [3] which was occasionally spoken by Ramana Maharshi to those who were distracted by events around them which were not connected to their desire for happiness.

Reminders like these exist because almost all the time, our thoughts make us forget our happiness is inside us. For millennia we have needed to be reminded to look inwards.

This was clearly known by the elders of the tribe; spiritual or religious leaders and even military leaders so let's look at this.

Roman

In Roman times, when victorious military commanders returned from battle, they took part in a public ceremony known as the 'Roman Triumph.' During the ceremony, standing just behind the victorious military commander was their servant who frequently whispered in their ear, 'Memento Mori,' (Remember you must die). This is one of the earliest instructions to remind us why we are here and also of the inevitability of death.

Judaism

Just as Christians use church bells as a call to prayer, on important occasions the Jewish call to prayer is made with a Shofar, a religious ritual instrument usually made of a ram's horn. However the routine call to prayer, 'Barekhu,' is recited at the beginning of the prayers at the beginning of daily morning and evening services. In Islam,

Islam

Muslims are called to prayer five times a day by the Adhan, which is sung, often broadcast loudly through public loudspeakers.

Daily prayers are private for Hindus, who traditionally pray in the mornings and for Buddhists who traditionally pray three times a day.

These multiple reminders given to us by the Angelus, Meditation, the Romans, the Barekhu or Adhan serve a single function. Their aim is to turn us away from thoughts, to turn us inwards, to just be.

Outer Securities - The Other Direction

Most of us are so conditioned and programmed by our families and educational systems to compete and achieve as high as possible educational standards and financial security that we over focus on thinking. We are lured to over-develop our thinking so much because we believe it will help us achieve our desire to acquire money, power, knowledge or influence, all of which we believe will make us happy.

We become so involved with thoughts; we actually see them as being us, instead of seeing them only like passing clouds in the sky.

We over identify with thoughts as actually being us instead of being only one of several aspects of us.

Focusing on thought is understandably necessary but only to the point of what is sufficient. If we choose to go beyond this point, led by our limited function of thinking, we travel further outwards, away from looking inwards and despite all efforts, we don't find happiness.

Eventually, after repeated disappointments we may see that happiness lies inside us and we can only find it by turning inwards.

So What Now

But what do we do after we stop and turn inwards? We know we can recite prayers, on our own or with others. We can use beads to count short prayers or special words. We can chant words. We can silently repeat a mantra. We can concentrate on our breath. But what are we doing and what are we trying to achieve with our thoughts and our consciousness?

Each of the above methods are preparations. They help us to move from our state of thinking to our state of being. They do this by reducing the number of thoughts we have down to just one thought, and then down to the state of having no thoughts, that is of just being conscious.

But what comes after these methods have slowed our thinking so we are 'almost' thought free?

Simple though this description may seem, not having thoughts is difficult because we are so used to having thoughts all of the time. Direct simple advice about how to do this, unshrouded by religious scripture or psychobabble, is extremely hard to find.

The Question of Consciousness

Looking at spiritual and religions paths both east and west there is a single shared thing to attend to, what is our meaning, what do we mean, who exactly are we. Our need to be fully conscious of who we are, what we are, goes back thousands of years.

This question 'Who am I' has been known by those in India, in Rome and elsewhere for millennia. It is first mentioned in the Book of Exodus. [4]

Moses asks the Burning Bush. "Suppose I go to the Israelites and say to them, 'The God of your fathers has sent me to you,' and they ask me, 'What is his name?' Then what shall I tell them?"

God said to Moses, "I am That I am. This is what you are to say to the Israelites: 'I am has sent me to you.'"

Perhaps this is the single shared core insight of spiritual paths.

If everything in the Universe comes from the same original material, then although a simplification, we could say that anything at all in the Universe, if it was able to answer the question of 'Who am I?' could in truth say, 'I am that.' Asked the same question, if a grain of sand or a mountain could speak, or if a Galaxy could speak, they could truthfully say, 'I am that.' Ourselves and the grain of sand speak truth as much as we can and maybe this is our limit of understanding our consciousness.

Essentially they both say our experience of who we think we are, our experience of ourselves as separate individuals is incorrect and that we are part of everything, or I am That.

The Multiverse

'I am That I am,' means our consciousness is the same as everything in the Universe and all else we think we are is secondary. It means we are part of a single unity, the Multiverse.

The Multiverse first described by Anaximander the Greek philosopher around 600 BC. [5] includes all space, all of time, all matter, and energy, the planets, stars and galaxies, other parallel Universes, all consciousness, everything known and unknown.

Giving up the belief that I am so and so, means removing our false sense of who we are i.e., that we are a bundle of thoughts called the ego.

In other words, we have to be the Universal self. The cosmic self. That is everything, the Multiverse. But we have to be it, not think about it because being is an experience not a thought.

Multiverse

Loss and love are one
Intertwined forever as one
Inseparable in tears and joy
Their union is life itself

The illusion of separate consciousness
Is like seeing river water
As it returns to the ocean
Being separate from the ocean

This can be troublesome to see as most of us are strangers to our Self because we have been conditioned or programmed to believe that what we consist of are memories of the past and fears and aspirations of the future i.e. that we are our thoughts.

Psychology cannot be used to understand this because psychology is limited by thinking, whereas consciousness is not limited by thought. This is because thought come from consciousness and not the other way around.

Conscious reasoning cannot understand this, so we are left only with our conscious intuition to understand. It is conscious intuition from empirical experiential knowledge.

Consciousness of the Goal is the Path

To return to our reminders, 'Being Still' and the inner enquiry of 'Who am I?' have been indirectly suggested in both art and writing over millennia by images and words.

Here are a few more reminders which show the unifying thread passed down through time in different countries in different forms, but always containing the same message about where to look.

Each one is an attempt to identify only what is essential, to remove our ignorance by stripping back everything else.

∞

One of the ancient Greek's key instructions, "Know the self." was written on one of the portals of their most important temple, the Temple of Apollo in Delphi 500-300 BC. [6]

∞

'Your duty is to be: and not to be this or that. "I AM that I AM" sums up the whole truth. The method is summed up in "BE STILL." [7]

∞

In the Upanishads 800-600 BC, 'Netti Netti' means, 'Neither this neither this,' which helps the mind to constantly negate and disidentify with anything other than that which is That. [8]

∞

A well-known Christian reminder is, 'Believe me, count as lost each day you have not used loving God,' [9] was written by Brother Lawrence a French monk in the mid-17th century.

∞

And again, Christianity helps to turn us inwards when in Luke it states, "The kingdom of God is within you." [10]

∞

Even Shakespeare pointed man strongly inside,' "This above all-to thine own self be true." [11]

∞

Summary

So, we have images of figures in the lotus meditation posture to remind us to be still. Also reminding us are the words from Aristotle, from the Upanishads, from the Hebrew Book of Exodus, from the Book of Psalms, from the Romans, from Luke in the Christian Bible, from Brother Lawrence and from Shakespeare. As well as these we have the reminders dividing up of the day by the Angelus, Barekhu and Adhan.

It doesn't matter which spiritual or religious path we have followed to get here, because it has got us here. Once we are here, following it or not makes little difference.

The unifying purpose of all of these paths is to experience consciousness of the bliss of being still, of being That.

References

1. Aristotle, Nicomachean Ethics, Book 1

2. https://indianculture.gov.in/museums/pash
   pati-seal

3. Nagamma, Suri, Letters from Sri Ramanas
   ramam, Volume II, Chapter 75, 16th
   February 1949.

4. Exodus 3:14

5. https://en.wikipedia.org/wiki/Anaximander

6. Temple of Apollo, Delphi, Greece

7. Sri Ramanasramam, Talks With Sri Ramana
   Maharshi 1994. Talk 363

8. Brihadaranyaka Upanishad 2.3.6

9. Brother Lawrence. The Practice of the
   Presence of God: With Spiritual Maxims.
   Forward by Mother Tessa Bielecki (Shambhala
   2015) P 121

10. Luke 17:20-21

11. William Shakespeare. Hamlet, Act 1, Scene 111.

∞

∞

∞

∞

∞

∞

∞

∞

$$\infty$$